Backhand Through the Mother

ALSO BY RENEE NORMAN

True Confessions (2005)
*House of Mirrors: Performing Autobiograph(icall)y in Language
    Education* (2001)

Backhand Through the Mother

poems by

Renee Norman

inanna poetry & fiction series

INANNA Publications and Education Inc.
Toronto, Canada

Canada Council   Conseil des Arts
for the Arts   du Canada

The publisher gratefully acknowledges the support of the Canada Council for the Arts for its publishing program.

Library and Archives Canada Cataloguing in Publication

Norman, Renee 1950-
  Backhand through the mother / Renee Norman

(Inanna poetry and fiction series)
Poems.
ISBN 978-0-9736709-9-8

1. Mothers and daughters—Poetry. I. Title.   II. Series.

PS8627.O77B32 2007   C811'.6   C2007-903502-7

Cover design by Valerie Fullard

Printed and bound in Canada

Inanna Publications and Education Inc.
210 Founders College, York University
4700 Keele Street
Toronto, Ontario, Canada M3J 1P3
Telephone: (416) 736-5356 Fax (416) 736-5765
Email: inanna@yorku.ca Website: www.yorku.cainanna

For my three daughters, again. Always.
And for my mother.

mother to daughter
daughter to mother
mother to daughter

your touch there
your print left
on the creak suck click tsk
sound of seconds
smoothed between us

Contents

Part I. Turning Point

Part II. Snail Slipping Off a Leaf

Part I: Turning Point

... the poems we live in ...

The Poem as Home

gather all the books & parcels
lines & stanzas
prayer shawls & smoking twists
of candles
fumble for the key

shoes kicked off
there is comfort
in the poems we live in
the beat of rhythms
skirt around the shadows
of Yawa prophets
cups of wine

I want to bring my poems
into the kitchen
cook them with the smells
of latkes frying
in family oil
roast chicken dipped
in children's laughter
doors & windows open
to draw the fresh rush
of worldly air

the poem as home
where suits & socks are shed
and songs that sing the skin
are written and mark the places
where we all come in

but home entraps too
for days on end
no language but your own
& silence does not answer
where the smells
grow stale

I need home and kitchens
to belong in poems that simmer
but where the words end
is where I next begin

4/4 Time in the Kitchen

heat from the vents
centres in the kitchen:
appliances played by hands
in a rhythm
lost if you don't notice
when the dials spin
the way the blades turn
how the doors fly
Lunch is ready!
food marks the minutes
of the day
steadies the family
in four four time
1   2   3   heat
from her 3   4
1   2   body WARNING
temperature too hot
reduce time by minutes
add more flour
when you double the tempo
in the kitchen
for the congregation
play this scale in C minor
your mind on other staves
each note builds
just the odd falter
measure wash season measure
structure to this repetition
there are memories in this rhythm
in her motion
the same heat from the vents
Lunch is ready!

Prodigal Mother

sometimes when I drive away
a daughter waving smiling sadly
from the window
the others invisible until
an extra arm or head
appear behind beside her
glass gargoyle gazing

I remember SueAnne
talked to me over our restaurant meal
spoke
about her husband and children
in Boston
still wondering about the day SueAnne
left
just a toothbrush in her purse
she never went back

I see SueAnne's sensitive stricken features
soft behind her eyes in her words
they know where I am now
if they ever need me
if they want to call

I was childless then
I didn't understand
all SueAnne could be
she gave birth at 19
too quickly in a toilet
then again a year later
she didn't like her husband

when I first drove away
for just an hour
I didn't like it
worried
the umbilical cord that tied me to my children
unsevered and secure

soon I learned to leave
longer times
worried less
needed to go
understanding I was not my children
we were joined but
separate too

these days I drive away
feeling freedom in my flight
fear
knowing all I've left behind
return
everyone rushes
to prodigal mother
returned to the fold
and I am grateful
relieved
I did not bring my toothbrush
like SueAnne

Daughters

against the stone wall
        youthful girlish bodies lean
                making plastic horses gallop
                        along the long ledge
                            of their fancy...

...today she turned away
  from my kiss
  the schoolroom door open
  & classmates gaping

  but tonight I will kiss her
        doubletime
        doubletime
  the notation of my love
  recorded on her cheek
            invisible
          permanent

Happy Birthday!

I'm not ready
for the big black Sony Space Sound radio
taking up half her dresser space
the classical tapes
returned to the stereo cabinet
Red Riding's Hood given away

I only just folded the diapers into dustcloths
dismantled the crib
donated small sleepers to the playroom dollhouse

I watch her
by her radio
still deep in thought
dreaming to the raucous music

I see myself
by the screen door
tears pouring down my eyes
I gaze out at prairie sunset
blood red dulled by summer haze
chequered in the tiny squares
of front door lookout
my mother's radio playing
songs that make me cry
apron tied
she dances round our kitchen
making dinner

I want to hide that radio
in her room

cover it
paint it white
unplug it
smash its speakers
glue the buttons down
give it away

but I won't
it's me there by the radio
the sunset's calling
it once spoke to me

I'll play her radio
dance around her room
put clothes away
tuned to a classical song I like
wish that radio wasn't there

Shit Work

toilet paper roll replacer
filtered water jug retopper
clothes refolder
toothpaste swisher
close-the-cupboard-doors

snack and lunch co-ordinator
used kleenex detonator
print remover
toilet flusher
turn-off-every-light

Barbie search and rescue captain
violence and sex detective
family rooster
in-house psychic
close-the-cupboard-doors

daily planner
form signer
time keeper
appointment maker
child minder
wound binder
turn-off-every-light

protect
    deflect
        detect
            inspect
advocate and engineer

save the planet
search and rescue
close-the-cupboard-doors

Grade 7 Graduation

a cultural emptiness
in the way they toss
their hair back
cross
their long lithe legs
in short flowered dresses
or overlong jeans

a cultural emptiness
in the goals & aspirations
of these postmodern children
who want to work
in the movie industry
to play
in the NBA
to make
lots of money
to be famous actors, famous models
famous cover girls, famous athletes

if anyone knows about
the women in Afghanistan
who had to cover themselves
from head to foot
whom the Taliban stoned to death
because they were walking with men

if anyone hopes to research cancer
stop clearcutting
love well
lead an exemplary life

it was not evident in their choice of words

how is it that we teach them
ancient civilizations & problem-solving skills
but not simplicity & the value of deep thought

who invited their Bart Simpson heroes
to sit among the parents & the teachers
snapping souls loose
with expensive cameras
the sound of electrons clapping

Knife in My Heart

first to go
snuggling in bed with me at night
she wants a dagger
for her middle school graduation present
(could just have the one in my heart)
her new clear braces
push her lips
even fuller in disapproval
all the decisions I make
she doesn't like
the nails of her two sucking fingers
now resplendent with black polish

I know this branching out
the cool distance
the tone in a reply
the place where the blade pierces
but I can't help missing
that warm body against mine
the sucking sounds

Into This Poem

I want to write
lush pink cherry blossoms
into this poem
the vivid green and yellow
of early spring
the joy at finding
the first red tulip in bloom
and the blue jays
helping themselves
to seed from the bird house

I want to write
the tousled head of my youngest
as she sucks 2 fingers
in repose
the I-love-you
of a 15-year-old
between bittersweet melodies
of the piano and flute
a 17-year-old
who still likes to come home
for lunch in her double block

I want to freeze memory
in this poem
     halt change
         erase time

but the squirrels
tear the roof off the bird house

and finish off the seeds
the fingers come out of the mouth
the melodies end
the school bell rings

Bird Watching

two pregnant stellar jays
guard the bird house my daughter has painted
(*Welcome Birds!*)
I have added some generic wild bird seed
in case they can't read

nearby a robin waits on another tree
watchful
I watch, too
this chain broken when the dog breaks loose
to bark hello at our neighbours

just back from Hong Kong
Mrs. Chin holds a Sears catalogue in her hand
& translates for Mr. Chin
the names of flowers we discuss over the retaining wall
that divides our yard
lilacs Japanese plum
rhododendrons   my three daughters
you are so lucky to have daughters
Mrs. Chin reminds me
they have only one son
"it is lonely" Mrs. Chin comments
Mr. Chin wonders if I should fertilize
the yellow plum tree

Segments

we are cutting the buns in half
the oranges into quarters
when I mention my youngest daughter
threw up 3 times the night before

it is then she tells me
the young heal quickly
your daughter will be fine
daughters are special
she loves her sons
but a daughter oh
a daughter

she had a daughter once
she quietly adds
one minute there at the dinner table
the next gone
and she could not accept that absence
that loss

my eyes fill with the crumbs
gathering on the tabletop
the juice released from sweet oranges
her split citrus pain

it is something
from which we never recover, I say
recalling my 2 miscarried babes
and the terrible joy of daughters
who are only ever on loan
from one moment to the next

we sweep the crumbs into a bag
she cuts the orange quarters smaller
even smaller

The Costume

I can't help laughing
don't sew
but know lop   when I see it
            sided
the next day down on my hands and knees
material spread out like a billboard poster
awaiting a message
I help her pull out more threads
pin   measure
  hunt   re-pin
the ungifted leading the eager
drawing upon the artistry of common sense
and love

at the machine
intent
head bowed like a woman in prayer
she runs the costume under the needle
that pinpricks the fabric lightly of this scene
she is so much more than me
a blessing in / at disguise

The Warm Blush

I think of it in colors:
the fluorescent orange of the pick-up truck
when he brought her to the school where I taught
the quilted pink of her long snowsuit
small feet poking through at knee point
the thin bluish-white of my milk
as it released into her expectant mouth
the two of us reunited in a bathroom

in the red and blue years
trucks became station wagons became jeeps
a never-ending fleet that signalled fecundity
or whim

alternating black or gold moods transformed that snowsuit
as it was reused then put away then used again
how much tone inflated the folds
until that suit got up and walked away
a stuffed cast doll bleating with desire
for the warm blush of baby flesh

    flash of orange
    blur of pink
I reach for
with outstretched hands

Checking My Daughters at Midnight
with Lotion on My Hands

night climbs over discarded clothes black jeans black camisole
with a trim of white lace under their eyelids other worlds move
across their faces quilts drawn up to nostrils like lilies
like peonies the fragrance of lilacs in the seams of open windows
let in the rush of air from the dark creek a woods lullaby
for those who sleep close to trees in the night's silence
an eloquent language of love and darkness heard between the sigh
of a deep dreamer the rustle of a body turned a fourth wall reflects
the hand smoothes the crease off a brow pain
of the whispered
of the whispered...

*Elemental, My Dear Poodle (or Proof
that One Can Try to Write a Poem About
Anything)*

no clean underwear
our once abundant supply
chewed by the dog
a potential poodophile
who seems to like
musky urinous smells
& works holes in places
meant to cover bodily apertures
from drafts

I like enough underwear
to stretch the week
no mad reaching on early school mornings

funny how underwear
undergirds our daily functions
unnerves us
when supply and demand don't match
each new day uncovered
by a fresh pair
of bright patterns or colors
hidden next to our skin
absorbing the smells
that so enthrall the dog
a perverted poodle
our undergarments fascinate him
the scent of little girls
women & bathrooms
blood: the material of life

soiled with smells
that permeate cloth
and like the dog chewing
remind us of the elemental

Caught!

hook in a trout's mouth
she calls excited
wants to let the creature loose
the cruel mangle of pin
an eagle swoops down
to grab
she so willing to relinquish

the eagle prepares her
for the futility of tenderness
but the trout
scales a glint of silver
struggling for air in light
strained through thick trees
blood staining the pocket
of her nylon jacket
(it holds a penny leaking red)

the trout tutors her
in the luxury of mercy

Anatomy of an Evil

aren't you afraid to wear that?
a grey-haired woman
with a heavy Jewish accent
points to my daughter's *magen david*
on a chain
no, my daughter retorts
with an attitude
black lipstick wild hair
trademark Adidas
and some boy's initials
carved on her hand in colored felt

I wear a *magen david,* too
point to mine around my neck
it's hidden, the old woman announces
my star under the collar of my shirt

it takes several generations
to learn not to flinch

Hannah's Child

would have been precocious
female of course
chattering away in German & English
before she let go of Hannah's desktop
to try walking

would have learned to scribble
quietly
while Mamala worked
filling papers with the dizzying marks
that fenced out a distance

loved
of course she would have been
a child of the republic
a light ahead of the dark times behind
more at ease with adults
whispering to her teddy
about Aunt Mary's blueberry pancakes

until she begged again
to hear the story of the Holocaust
a family album of never forget
this page Buba Martha
sounding strict
turn over to someone named Walter Benjamin
the sad pallor of suicide
in the tone of voice
a puzzle
when she pointed to a framed picture
of Uncle Martin on the desk

& in the way that children can
imaged a second picture there
in her mother's measured reply
black & shadowy like a silhouette

*Aunt Mary is Mary McCarthy
Uncle Martin is Martin Heidegger
Buba Martha is Martha Arendt, Hannah Arendt's mother

Mother Troll

suddenly
I am the enemy
a troll
(her word not mine)
who rampages through private diaries
plunges through boxes of keepsakes
aims bug-out eyes over to the letters
crawling on the computer screen
grabbing secrets

the truth of the matter
is both more and less than that
a desire to understand and keep connected
a spilled gathering of memorabilia
beneath the changing of the sheets
a page left open that beckons
(read me)

mother troll
is not just rifling through scraps of memory
trying to steal the soul
out of teenage independence

she is making beds of netting
a place for both of us to fall upon
when blankets fray
and holes open wide
to painful words

Absence

no,
she doesn't want to be
in the picture
by the lake
the pink sky alight
with watercolour brightness

her sisters sit on the bench
agreeable they wait for release
and a flash of more light

she is afraid
I will be taking part of her
away with the camera
I don't argue her right
to stand on sidelines
a lone sad figure in black

but she is wrong
I do not suck up flesh or image
nor with an xray lens
probe the deepest secrets
that she harbours in her solitude

instead I try
to put my arms around this moment
still her dark hurt
heal the memory

Metal Flowers

slowly I notice
the long ramp which leads
to your back door
the piece of black equipment
resting on the table
metal flowers
the warning label on
the back of the wheelchair
the way you seem to
know what he wants
with no word spoken
the steady stream of
therapists & caretakers & visitors
which you conduct as
you take the cups from the dishwasher
for our tea
how you pull his wheelchair
up to the table
while we drink our tea
include him in our conversation
the tender kiss you apologize for
because he is 16
as you stand him
leaning on your knees
for support
the root beer
which you pour down
his throat
advising me
with a laugh
to move

& dabbing at
whatever spurts
out the corners

your other child
shows me a school project
but my eyes
travel over to
you adjusting food in
his mouth
and your eyes meet mine
in a curious mixture
of defiance & resignation
& I notice then

you are the poet
composing profound images of love
with easy gestures

Bearing Witness September 12, 2001

for years
torn as I worried
were my daughters safe?
I drove out of my home world
into another
seeking stimulation
adult conversation
a life of the mind

at first I fussed
was the babysitter kind
cautious
did she know to keep doll shoes
out of mouths
and cut the grapes

then entrusting them to schools
kissing them at classroom doors
I prayed for close supervision
and the patience of angels

now I accept
that to be alive is enough
to come through the door
find everyone accounted for
an incredible gift
the leaving still as hard as ever
the return
oh so much sweeter

When the Oldest Gets Her Driver's License at Last

what is this new feeling?
gratitude?
someone else to drive
and buy the blueberries
relief?
I don't have to return the overdue video
joy?
some time to stay still
reflect
the constant back and forth motion
slows from motor vehicle
to rocking chair
I am no longer chauffeur to whims
(ice cream, movie, sunglasses, thong underwear)
what is this new feeling?

worry
worry
loss

Performing: Adolescent Getting Ready for School

in the morning
she paints herself
into the room
a palette of powders
blush   eyeliner   sparkles
coat face and counter

a gossamer shirt
she has applied
to long flowing skirt
holds the embrace
of golden bodice
the expression almost complete

if you approach
when she is forming
the pain of the process
forces harsh tones
from ruby lips

watch
still and quiet
and shape transforms
as she drifts past
the spring of drawn curls
drying water in heat
from morning air registers

reach to touch
her eager decoration
the taste of hope

delicious
in the folds of color
outlined in black depths

each day she returns
re-painted
by the mood of those she passes
invisible to some
she burns others with her brand
of isolated beauty

First Night of Chanukah

these days makeup stains the counters
by the sink an assortment of products
announces the individual
tone drips in a simple reply
and my good road record disappears
when a driving princess is passenger to my decisions

these days a poem written for school
must never be shown to me
details about boys filter
to me only as the residue of what is overheard
and as soon as I pick up the phone
I am quickly dismissed from existence

but when it came time to light the candles
the first night
all of us gathered in the glow
of brass, wax, flame,
we sang the ancient words that connect us
the heat of the melody intense
alighting childhood in our eyes
and love, too, remembrance,
the memory of melting

Car Keys

the power has shifted
I am ordered to keep the car keys
on the hall desk

we are entering new territory
cultivated by burgeoning independence
a more equal sorority

I see the turns in those new roads
feel some relief
the unfurling of burdens
time and care
but mostly
loss

you can't tuck in a young woman
who moonlights till 2 AM
so I remove eyeglasses
turn off the TV
in the heat of a noon day

slip the keys into my purse

Grade 12 Graduation

this empty room
signifying change
how did my mother do it?
that terrible silence

you never sever
the bodily connection
but it's hard to look
at the trophies on the wall
the air full of practised notes
and not feel some beat of sadness
as I sort her dirty clothes
while she registers for courses
in another city

I am amazed
how one person less
makes such a difference
these ghostly garments
obviously make an impression
but the hollow place in me
is naked

Emptying the Nest (Eldest Daughter Moves Out, 2 to Go)

I won't miss the 5 pairs of shoes in the front hall
the clothes drying in the laundry room
all week long until I finally remove them
the eyes rolling as she turns
thinking I don't see that because
I'm so old, so stupid, so--everything!

I won't miss her clutter spread out all over her bedroom floor
and radiating into the rest of the house
the extra charges on the credit card
waiting half-asleep for the front door
to open at 2 AM
the unwiped cupboards, the dishes left for me
long after supper has been cleared away

you weren't so great yourself,
my mother reminds me
and I'm beginning to understand why
my mother gave all the photos back
refuses to accept plants as presents
she doesn't want to nurture so much as a leaf anymore

but I will miss that tall body lying beside me in bed
while we watch a video at night
or discuss her latest love interest
and how the hell will I ever learn to burn a CD
or install anti-virus
and no matter how much time is now returned to me
how much I love to hear myself think in the much neater quiet
traded for a vibrant young woman's noise

I'll keep wondering if I hugged her enough
if I savoured every passing stage
if I'll recognize myself in her poems

So Who's Bulemic Here?

no sugar allowed, we claim
my daughters and I buy
sugarless peanut butter
sugarless jam
ice cream with Splenda
Boticelli chocolate with maltitol
sugarless revels
and gummy bears from the diabetics section
our orange juice is unsweetened
our fridge crammed with fresh fruits and veggies
the cupboard is stocked with fruit to go's and gum
and we hide the licorice that my husband
can't seem to resist

it's war on white refined
and brown too
Atkins
LA Weight Loss
calorie counting
South Beach
you name it
we've tried it
sometimes all at once
like Bridget Jones
we're in the zone man
we mean business
ignore the raised eyebrows at the checkout
the extra trips to the bathroom
and not just to check that inaccurate scale either

we barter the last of our allotted bars

for almost anything
increasingly desperate
wail over who finished the last of the ice cream
and so far
no one knows
that I always stash a few fruit to go's
in my school knapsack
or else I never get any

we know we are better off without sugar
yes
much better off
cleansing our bodies
(the aftereffects of maltitol?)
and when our manic cycle repeats itself
again and again
we feel secure in the knowledge
there are no eating disorders in this family

Garage Sale

behind the old woman who stoops
even lower to plug in & test
an old hot plate ($2)

a couple swoops toys into bags
for their new daycare
(we'll give you $25)

others inquire about parts:
cameras, cars, bikes
all the internal organs
of machinery that has gaps

there is a culture here at work
in the bathing suit straps
stiff with dried sunscreen (25 cents)
in the 6 glass saucers
with no cups (50 cents)
& the old orange syrup jar
which has never felt sticky liquid (10 cents)

consider:
how surprised Mr. Potato Head will be ($5)
to wake up in a bag
& stare out his newly placed eyes
at someone else's offspring

how the woman whose baby was due
in 1 week
will labour as she rolls hard dough

with the red-handled pin
(free with the $25 vacuum)

how the couple who left behind
the bolt for the old vertical blinds ($10)
will look & look for a way to hang the rod

Moth into Flame

the giant Atlas moth
its wingspan
the length of a grade school ruler
spends 3 to 5 years
reaching maturity
and then –
in a blaze of color
shapes smells tastes
sensations
lives only 3 to 5 days
ah, the intensity of adulthood
the burden of wings

Between the Lines

what's wrong with your hands?
she asks as I grip the steering wheel

how to answer a child
who writes madly, deeply
about a boy she barely knows?

a veneer of tracks
I had not noticed until now
drives over my skin

do I reply:
my skin's wrinkling,
the elasticity's gone,
it's soybean time,
it'll happen to you,
watch the sun,
watch the road,
watch what you read in those girls' magazines?

instead I say my hands are dry
I need some cream
(and cosmetic surgery and
soft lights and
trick mirrors and
a time machine)

it is a turning point
all day I check my hands
rub in lotions
make the lines disappear

Part II: Snail Slipping Off a Leaf

... echoes deafening in the freefall ...

Backhand Through the Mother

the blur of nights
when all else
asleep
the two of us
rocked
in the creak suck sound of minutes
wanting
her to finish
one part drifting off to sleep
each draw and suck a shock
of body pleasure

you passed me hot cloths
early morning hours
knew my pain
sought to ease
the crust
hot compresses drew
my reluctant milk
softened
the click tsk sound of seconds

you cooked scrubbed organized
red raw hands
dry folds of skin
crooked index finger
(never properly healed)
shook
your fatigue pointed out
my dependence gratitude
guilt

my hands
dry folds of skin
hold pass cook
scrub organize
mother to daughter
daughter to mother
mother to daughter
your touch there
your print left
on the creak suck click tsk
sound of seconds
smoothed between us

4 loads of laundry

hang in the sun
3 generations of women
pin unpin
the nightgowns
to   from
the line

First Generation
your lips purse
at a sycophantic salesclerk
when you buy me a new gown
I notice how your cheeks sink
how you hang the wet clothes upside down

Second Generation
I examine the clothes
to see if they are dry
the skin on my hands is parched
lined with creases
that cross between mothers and children and nightgowns
whose hems gently stir
at the push from a breeze

Third Generation
your gums show a large tear
where 2 permanent teeth rip through
barely do you have the strength
to open a clothespin
and throw the clothes unfolded
like paper dolls into baskets

that once you climbed inside
4 loads of laundry hang in the sun
in the sun

Hybrid Clotheslines

I dream of clotheslines
strung out
northwest Calgary yards
my grandfather's apartment building
across prairie
hybrid clotheslines
of memory

I am always hanging on them
sheets and towels mostly
pulley clotheslines that never end
flying   flapping
remnants of childhood
and long wooden porches

Oxen on the Roof

under the glass
a faded sepia photograph
of my grandfather Aaron
is preserved
a reflection of a Jewish Czechoslovakian man
riding a bicycle
smiling
in the foreground
behind him an ox upon the roof
trapped in picture memory time
upon a Yastrap village house

underneath my coffeetable glass
my grandfather (Zeda)
on the bicycle
rides freely
year after year
protected from the dust
of another generation
viewing
the oxen helpless on the roof
   my grandfather helpless on the roof
      the oxen helpless on the bed
         my grandfather helpless on the bed

my mother maneuvres the spoon
to Zeda's dry caked lips
a rhythm in her feeding frenzy
rife with long-forgotten spoonfed strokes
his old mouth involuntarily

opens to receive masticated sustenance
upon a cot-size bed
mushy life-giving motion delivered
on the silverware of daughterly devotion

I listen
focus on the rivulets of spoonfed spittle
and dripping streams of soft oatmeal-colored mush
disgustingly displayed
my grandfather's countenance
a mask of helpless hopeless
painted streaks of food
lifeless eyes staring
through the food framed face
an old baby
tableturned in the mirror
to a mothering daughter

Do you remember Renee, Dad?
She's home for the summer
Come to see you
Open wide
That's good
He eats well, you know
It's what keeps him going
All these years
We cried, all of us
There you go
When we sat in the office
We couldn't do it any more
It wasn't fair to Rose

Just a few more spoonfuls
Rose and I take turns
Coming to feed him
They haven't the patience here that we do
Don't give it back to me, Dad, that's better
Although they're very good
Lucille visits
Cec too
I know Irene will help
When they've moved
Now you're finished, wasn't that good?
Not all the grandchildren come to visit

in the presence of my mother's daughterly spirit
myself a daughter to her motherly magic
I cast a spell of backward time
upon that dear old foodstained face
clean it with a cloth of memory
place it upright upon a couch in my living room past
watch its mouth spilling spellbinding stories
of other countries
officers and wars
and ships that sailed away from our ancestral destruction

I'll tell you since you ask, Reevkala
We lived in a little village
Yastrap
It exists no more
I knew another war was coming
I was twice already an officer for the Germans
I speak seven languages, sheyna medelah

And I thought, no more, too many times
I could see what was coming
Max and I came over first
It took us five years to save the money for the others
Your mother was a baby when I left
A few days old
The youngest of seven
Although one other baby died
A more beautiful baby than your mother
I have never seen
Max is the oldest
I brought him with me
It wasn't good for him
A black sheep you might say
He broke your grandmother Sarah's heart
Sarah, God rest her soul
Would not speak of him
Even when she was dying
  Even when I was dying
    Even when I was the oxen on the bed
      Even when I was the oxen on the roof

underneath the glass
my grandfather Aaron still rides
his bicycle
past the oxen on the roof

Black Sheep

toss grain to chickens
(predictable pecking)
pick some dill
a large patch of weedy green
spiked spindles
(remember Sarah's pickles)
thin the huge clumps of rhubarb
spreading large spanned leaves
upward in supplication
to a blue sky
(remember Sarah's pies)
sigh
breathe the summer air
herbal scent of pickles-to-be
spice of imaginary pies
a baby wails
hungry
gaze upward
back porches lined with
diapers shirts pants dresses
underwear
drying in the breeze
flat empty garments
whisper the secrets
of the lives that fill them out
touch the wrench
in back pocket
signal a silent note:
repair the taps
remember your oldest son
shake this out

put it away
like the clothes reeled in
off the clotheslines
like the rhubarb steaming
in the pies
like the dill pickling
in the jars
chickens pecking
pecking

Prayers for the Almost Dead

a devil wind
whips up in a hot prairie field
carries away
whatever is not weighted down
by the gravity of childhood

while peonies full of ants
bow low to the dry cracks in the earth
davening like old Jewish men
in a mournful prayer for the almost dead

who read the morning newspaper (a beloved routine)
with a magnifying glass

black marks the ants
move across an insect page
an infinitesimal funeral march

More Prayers for the Almost Dead

asleep
mouth open, slack
a view up her 2 dark nostrils
it slaps me
the force of a branch whipped across a picture window
she is old

every good day is extra
cook some chicken
trim the Weigela
vacuum the rug
to hold onto living
a lifeline of menial tasks

yeesgadal v'yeesgadash
the retina has separated from the eye
yeesgadal v'yeesgadash
I want to work until I can't
yeesgadal v'yeesgadash
the stomach's blocked
yeesgadal v'yeesgadash
don't take me to the hospital

yeesgadal v'yeesgadash
kaddish prayers for the almost dead

sh'mai raba

Crazed Cookies

my mother
         expecting death
baked sesame twist cookies all morning
waiting for the phone to ring
answering machine turned to off

my mother
         recognizing death
in the hospital waiting room
went home and
feeling nervous
worked in her blue kitchen
where she knew the phone would ring
as surely as the tulips lost
their petals to the wind
every springtime

my mother
         foreshadowing death
filled her freezer with those cookies
rows of twisted dough corpses
packed in shoebox coffins
defrosting them
only two days later

my mother
        no stranger, she said, to death
served those cookies
cleared the plates that held them
vacuumed sesame seeds from
rug corners
and said,
prepare yourself
but don't let it make you crazy

Summer Fragments

at the entrance to Calgary's Exhibition Park
3 magpies under a tree scold each other
between the trees swarms of tiny black flies
fill people's mouths
all week there has been the threat of thunderstorms
& no sign of lightning
except on a golf course in Pigeon Lake, Alberta
a bolt entered a man's foot and surged through his shoulder
(imagine his handicap)
as we absorb the heavy summer tension
my aunt will die on the operating table
an uncle who breathes with an oxygen tank
defies death hourly
and my father's circulation isn't reaching
to his toes

past the pencil-shaped poles of an old fort
writing destinies in clouds of black
my head replays fragments of conversations
                    they don't care when you're old
                    you wouldn't want to see her so emaciated
                    I hope I go quickly
                    if she goes, she goes

on the midway daredevils are released into the heavens
on a rope extended like an elastic
we hit the balloon with the dart & win a prize
every player wins
we pat Shetland ponies
Tennessee Walkers, Arabians

the soil, a paste of sweat & dust
comes off on our palms
while a horse spreads his front legs to relieve himself

> *when he passes away, I'll have the surgery*
> *it's part of the territory*
> *so you'll see a vascular guy*
> *don't toss the baby in the air,*
> *it's very dangerous*

when we leave the park
the smell of no rain in the air

> *I'm holding*
> *while he goes to the upstairs phone*
> *it takes him forever*

the magpies have disappeared under the plush lower boughs
of the tree
we know they are there

Fred and Ginger at 80

my mother is my father's legs
rushing to fetch
a plate-a pickle-his cane-his pills
she cannot move fast enough
to taste her own food
before he barks another order
shouting at her body
to move nimbly
make up for what he's lost

mostly she bites her tongue
and obeys
dances in and out of the kitchen
the frustration

i think they both know
people don't dance forever

Photograph

it is the summer
my father sits on a lawnchair
his cane beside him
(benevolent patriarch on plastic throne)
my husband restrings the circular clothesline
so my mother can hang laundry
as she has every summer
for 38 years in this house

they make a tableau
juxtaposed by my watchfulness
father overseeing
son-in-law overseeing
clothesline   *c l i c k !*
a picture

but the string will not co-operate
and all the lines hang low
38 years, the clothesline creaks and groans
and no amount of adjusting
will make the strings taut

my mother's sheets
will touch the ground
all too soon
my father's cane will topple
my watchfulness
will turn to grieving
revolving in the tension
of old clotheslines

and all that will be left
is the photograph
the dirt stains

Checkup

see you next year
the eye doctor's receptionist
calls gaily to my father

when a water droplet spills
on calligraphy letters
they run and blur
is this how it all ends?
indistinct markings
glib goodbyes

I hope so, my father wryly replies
facing death with good vision
black humour
he sees the future clearly
in a dark sentence

Learning Death

on the phone my mother pauses
tells my father: breathe deep, Joe,
take a deep breath
the labour of death
my father hiccups again
gasping for air
his liver de-livering
yet another blow to the body
minute by minute heaving

on the phone my sister says
dad has passed away
this time the background noise
is our weeping
is there anything else I can do for you?
the ticket agent asks
can you cure cancer?

in the limousine
my mother   brother   sisters sit
a family reunion?
we're going out for Chinese!
but my father's in the trunk
you look good, one sister said
before the limo arrived
death agrees with me

at the chapel
the rabbi tears a black ribbon
pins it on my left shoulder
we sit between the kleenex boxes

what is left of my father's body
in a thin box draped with magen davids and cloth
is this grief or jet lag?

at the cemetary I shovel
dirt on my father's coffin
memorize the sound of soil
the grave open, a rectangular mouth
howling wind and snow
this is a movie funeral
the colour of ice

in synagogue
the words of the Mourner's Kaddish
tangle my tongue
yeesgadal v'yeesgadash   sh'mai raba
in awkward memory
of other times
other mourners
my childish unacceptance
finally shaken

above the earth I fly
my father's grave is covered
with small gritty scoops of everyone
his pipes and hats
in my suitcase
the remnants of childhood

I am high in the air
at the top of the ferris wheel

my father has taken me to the fair
the seat rocks in delicious terror
back and forth

The Literacy of Loss

I'm going to miss Zeda
my daughter
has learned death this past year
in 5 simple words
she captures the lesson

I don't know
how to teach her
to fill the empty chair in December
or walk along the beach again
without feeling she has lost summer

so I will tutor her
in new rituals and other oceans
introduce the fine ring of crystal
and exotic seashells
put to the ear
instruct her to heed the echoes

My Father's Pen

writing words
I hold my father's pen
I know the ink will not last forever
poetry sucks it dry

but I need to write sorrow
with his imprint
close to what he felt in the end
when he knew
"maybe later"
meant right now
when I knew
I love you
was good-bye
my father's pen
the instrument of memory

The Widows

they fall asleep glasses still on
and teeth out   face fallen in on itself
portable phone between the folds of bed
in houses much too big for sole occupant

at card games
they partner one another
to make foursomes
remember all too well
the ghost on the empty chair

when someone else dies
they are there at 2 AM
making phone calls
bringing casseroles
picking out cemetery plots
reliving this passage as a friend

they have learned
how to shop small
cook light
keep things in place
as they could never do before

bridge and golf connect them
this network of women
who know what it is to be alone
how to keep memory alive
watching his TV shows
wearing a leather jacket far too big
and saying again and again

he enjoyed the garden
and that's the only reason why I planted it
how he loved California strawberries
and only the pockets of the suit he was last wearing
had any papers in it

Legacy

don't get old
my mother warns
on the phone
is there a choice?

I hear my father's absence
in her voice
afraid to ask
wonder who changes the light bulbs
my sadness alive
in the particular

her widow world is bridge
blood tests
golf
skating on TV
the figures bleed across the ice
in perfect form
triple axles
and long programs
pushing the air
with supple youth
only a fall
reminds us
don't get old

sometimes I watch
blades cut ice
miles away
my mother views
the same cold marks

and I think about my daughters
thinking about me
a long legacy
of matriarchal power
this mind mapping
the love
the arguments
our day-to-dayness

we will not get old, mother
will skate and skate
we will not fall
and when a light burns out
our daughters will blaze on ice

Snail Symmetry

all the way to school
they pick up snails
place them out of harm's way
on a bush   a leaf
a lawn
o, the crunch a foot makes
when sole unintentionally meets
thin crust of shell

sitting in a living room
over tea and get-to-know-you-chatter
the health of respective elderly parents
comes up
o, the thump of one dropped shoe
followed by the bottomless hollow
of a silent leather mate

they seem slow, snails
inching their way to the edge of curbs
or into children's hearts

so soon the sound of silent footsteps
echoes deafening in the freefall

snail slipping off a leaf

Eye of the Needle

I'm lonely, my mother admits
a year after my father died
there's nothing here for me, she claims
an itinerant visitor
I worry when we walk on ice
put my hand out
but she waves it away

she lives
between a regimen
of pills and eyedrops
clever meals for one
a spotless house
4 or 5 items bought
on an outing
filling the day
with small ordinary tasks
that used to number 100

the pace is measured
but every incorrect bank statement
or memory of the past year
upsets her
then she sleeps only with a pill
suspended in widowhood
in a state of insecurity

we talk and talk
eat tidy meals
between the eyedrops
I thread 4 needles for future use

when I return to my life
I count the shoes
strewn all over the garage porch
with 20/20 vision
stock the fridge
as if preparing for disaster
spin 1000 former irritants
into an intricate tapestry of blessings

Apple Harvest

the apples are ready for picking
the smell of summer's end
the colour of another beginning

all afternoon my daughters peel and cut and laugh
screaming when an earwig leaps out
soon they will go their separate ways
one daughter laments: I don't even like apple pie!
layers of peel rise--a compost--on the tabletop
along with love, regret
summer's bittersweet cider
the neat bags of apples their gift to me
all my years of time and service
tart like the apples they cut,
removing the rotten parts

another harvest
this labour of apples
this fruit I love

Every 4200 Years

above the room
where my mother & I talk
the Hale-Bopp comet makes its appearance
for another night
I am eager to spot it
before it disappears from view
for another 4200 years

my mother has just put corrective drops
in her eyes
she doesn't care for comets
her vision is inward
streams of viscous tears rain down her cheeks
I don't know how many more times
her eyedrops will turn to salt

my yellow words light a sodium comet in the room
and one of Hale-Bopp's tails
wags a trail of dust through the universe

Loving Others: the Finest Act, the Riskiest

years & years in the same house
then something else goes:
the stove element
a friend's breast
the tiles are loose by the front door
next: a uterus? a clock? a bowel?

who will break
& what will wear out next?
that phone call very late at night
--just a wrong number
stops the heart
temporality calls daily

driving away from my house
I pray for a return trip
& new linoleum to cover the old
I want another year
without bi-focals or *yirzat* for the dead
I don't want to conjure up more
children navigating crosswalks
motherless
where I pause

New Year: Restructuring My Fantasies

a figure in black
a poetic silhouette
down an onyx corridor of darkness
the door opens
to long coattails and hair
it is the future

every day I check the horoscopes
for something that fits the way I feel
seize the hopeful predictions
concentrate all thought
to what might be
restructure my fantasies

year of the boar
soars
in future's shadow

Warm Spots

a look passes
between us
the old woman in the wheelchair watches
submerged in the pool
as I caution my wildly splashing daughter
not to bump her

it is more than a gaze
which enters me & signifies silent sorrow:
my body is light in this pool
not the burden it has become to me
I am weightless here
the wind flying through the trees
I am the white foam on the crest
touch me & I disappear
a warm spot in the water

meanwhile along the pole of a tree
the 2-toed sloth
dances its slow dance
a desperate movement
it is more than a dance
from branch to branch
1 2
claw on branch
3 4
slow rhythmic turn
touch it & it disappears
a warm spot in the air

Turning 50

when I turn 50
I will take naps
repeat myself
forget words, names, details
repeat myself
forget...
nap...

NO!

when I turn 50
I will begin a new career
    (sit on stone walls waiting for the bus to come)
write a poem everyday
    (run only when my hip doesn't hurt)
try to get a second book published
    (try to eat less and only when I'm hungry)
go to conferences in exotic locales
    (pack comfortable shoes)
not care anymore that I'll never be thin
    (not look in mirrors at my chin)

A LITTLE MORE POSITIVE, PLEASE~

when I turn 50
I will think about
women who give birth at 63
Gloria Steinhem's marriage
how I felt when I received my doctorate at 49
the oldest living woman who is 125 years old
how long it takes to print my cv
how long it takes to print my cv

Never Too Late

for years
I've gone barefoot in my house
prefer the cold
shock of floor
feet firm on tiled ground
as life slips by
a scatter rug

and then this pair of slippers
soft, deerbrown
my feet disappear
into the present
a gift of keen perception
inaccurate really
but oh so true

I've been haughty
over the years
minimized others' contributions
but I'm learning the value
of covered soles
and dedication
the quiet tread
of humility

Recipe for Reciprocation

with even strokes
my mother brushes the phyllo leaf
with melted butter
exclaims her delight
that she is learning something new

her leathery hands
lift the papery sheet
as carefully as a newborn
lay it tenderly over the filling
and lovingly pat it into place
if I close my eyes
I swear a hear a burp released

I am teaching her
a new trick
the thin parchment dries quickly
as we work
this edible papyrus
exotic to her at 75

and each time I explain
the next step
advise   encourage
praise   applaud
I marvel that it is me
mothering my mother

at last I return
a small piece of devotion
in Greek spinach pie

Acknowledgements

Thank you to my family for their enduring, good-natured responses to my fascination with both autobiographical writing and poetry, and for allowing me to write about them and share it with the world. And thank you, Don, and daughters Sara, Rebecca, Erin, for your tolerance and humour, which has ranged from "And don't write about this in one of your poems!" to "I smell a poem coming!" Additional thank yous: To my wonderful editor, Luciana Ricciutelli, for her support and her vision. To Carl Leggo, who first encouraged me to seek publication for my writing and who has been a supportive friend ever since. To George McWhirter, who taught me how to turn words poetically and who understood what I was trying to say in my poems even when I did not. To the women whose words I have read and reread, absorbed and valued. To women everywhere, whose tears are counted, and whose ordinary lives matter and are worth writing about. To mothers and daughters and sisters, the most complex of relationships and so dear. And to Tux, who for the thirteen years of his poodle life, has waited patiently and loyally by my side as I worked with words, hoping it would soon be time for a walk.

Some of these poems have appeared in their current or slightly altered form in the following journals and periodicals:

Canadian Woman Studies, Association for Research in Mothering Journal, The Missing Line Anthology, Child Anthology, Our SchoolsOur Selves, English Quarterly, Green Magazine, Room of One's Own, Amethyst Review, Prairie Journal, Kaleidoscope Magazine, Freefall Magazine, lichen, Whetstone, Writing for Our Lives, Wreck, Surrey International Writers Contest Anthology, Dandelion, People's Poetry Letter.

"Segments" won second place in the Southwest Regional Contest.

"Metal Flowers" received third prize in the Indiana Poetry Contest.

"Snail Symmetry" won honourable mention in the Surrey International Writers Contest.

"Recipe for Reciprocation" received honourable mention in the *Freefall Magazine* Contest.

"Grade 7 Graduation" received honourable mention in the Hope Poetry Contest.

Renee Norman, Ph.D., is an award-winning poet, a writer, and a teacher. Her first volume of poetry, *True Confessions,* was awarded the prestigious Helen and Stan Vine Canadian Jewish Book Award for Poetry in 2006. Her doctoral dissertation, *House of Mirrors: Performing Autobiograph(icall)y in Language/Education*, received the Canadian Association for Curriculum Studies Distinguished Dissertation Award and was published in 2001 (Peter Lang). Renee's poetry, stories, and articles have been published widely in literary and academic journals, anthologies and newspapers. Currently, Renee is a faculty member at University College of the Fraser Valley in the Teacher Education Program. She lives in Coquitlam, British Columbia, with her daughters and husband.

MEMBER OF SCABRINI GROUP

Québec, Canada
2007